TUXEDO

POEMS BY TAD CORNELL

Juggling Teacups Press
Kintnersville, Pennsylvania

ISBN: 978-0-9908633-6-6

tadcornell6331@gmail.com
tadcornell.com

Juggling Teacups Press
Kintnersville, Pennsylvania

"The literary critic must also be, at least, a metaphysician, but not just any metaphysics will do. The long theological-metaphysical tradition that begins with the ancient Greeks and careens smoothly on through history until the modern philosophers tried to shipwreck it, must be restored its deserved authority. Only in that tradition, the Christian-Platonist tradition broadly construed, where beauty is understood as knit into reality, perhaps even constitutive of it, can literary criticism flourish. And only, to repeat, if critics have the intelligence and education to argue persuasively within that tradition, can their practices have any claim on our souls, can they worthily support our incontestable and insatiable vocation to the contemplation of the Real."

—James Matthew Wilson

The Fortunes of Poetry in an Age of Unmaking

CONTENTS

The great geniuses of the past still rule over
us from their graves; they still stalk or scurry
about in the present, tripping up the living,
mysteriously congesting the traffic, confusing
values in art and manners, a brilliant cohort of
mortals determined not to die,
in possession of the land.

—Wyndham Lewis (1915)

TUXEDO

PART I

TUXEDO

When she sings, you're back in your cradle
reveling in how loss and hope can chime
with perfect blend in sleep's shadows.

Swaddled is a boon for the rich in mulch.
To know yourself as seed deposited
amid an anthem of harvest, or dirge

that claims a catastrophe you earned,
both bring solace in nakedness.
She promises no future grand tuxedo.

The puzzling sight of masks designed
to stimulate a clutch still dangles,
now ignored within her lullaby.

Sweet intuition flinches from use,
from sheer utility, and meaning
floats the boat of founding research.

THE DRIFT

Tuxedo goose-steps on old newsreels
sunk in Adolf's empire-style graphics
realized in actual film, hailing studs.

Emotiveness is slime on useful shafts.
Bow tie straps the neck with greedy hands.
Publishers Clearing House has found you.

The drift as History Channel plays
is loss of consciousness called sleep.
But in that netherness, a land is known.

In this world cruel masquerade is fun,
or maybe code for some internal school
that only goatherds could decode.

Characters are filing past the camera,
Lockean and Kantian, locked arms
of Rousseau and Adam Smith singing.

WESTERNS

Westerns are sleeping's best screen.
The dialogue is always rooted firm
in archetypes. No deciphered script

is needed for the tango sleep demands.
Other films explode to wake the dead
punctuating some seductive quiet calm.

Nightmares are born in storms like these.
Westerns, yes, the shootout comes
and desperate hand to hand is read

inside friend Freud's laboratory.
But it reads with odd harmony.
Don Quixote is taken seriously here.

The challenge is met in real time
within your dream. The dragon
has not yet lost its Eden legs.

CHARACTERS

So characters emerge as thought
devoid of context, sinking as if
in quicksand, dreaded by explorers.

Each brings an urgent memo
that embodies social content scheme
that always predicts perfectly

the sense in utter nonsense claimed.
You'd think at least they'd throw a vine.
They seem to sink with you as voices

sailing like the Thunderbird
they say is lord of northern skies.
No less than Berkeley, Butler, and Hume

have found in you a cosmic mash.
Northern lights and southern hemisphere's
winter solstice collide. Tuxedo haunts.

YOUNG ELOISE

Words have no meaning. The decision struck
the nation like news of Little Big Horn.
The IRS is now the captain of your scalping.

But worse is alien virus, absence of reason
as based in criterion, patiently building
our own asylum for the always manipulated

padded cell of prejudice and preference.
Sinking into sleep, you see yourself weeding
with young Eloise and teaching full

disclosure of the crimes and glories
that brought us here knowing that
a war declared long since is here today.

What a knowing pillow hugs these jowls!
You grope for history's fine points
in your sideways ripple of torn roots.

MIRRORED SHOES

The tuxedo is a trusted police informant.
It's eyes are in its neck and it walks
on mirrored shoes. You smell a rat.

Bifurcation is the norm for such as
these, the wardrobe set, monogrammed
and strapped to no possible scrutiny.

Worse than a modern poem, moral speak
has murdered strides in moral walk
we knew as rational criteria, murdered

all but rabbit trick ultimate principles
used only for skilled closing of debate.
Society at last has mastered sleepwalking.

Salvador Dali would be impressed,
especially the part about mirrored shoes
and absent heads from formal threads.

PRIMORDIAL ACT

The primordial act of experience
opens the door with butler calm.
He is gloved in numinous white.

Could reality by the senses truly
deserve a dignity so grand,
so godlike, so capable of mind?

Does it require descent into Styx
with all life's fragments bleeding
to know the way to that door?

Someone proposes trust in love.
The words of this equation, are they
what guides our waking hours?

Lewisburg Federal Penitentiary
was founded in a Gothic humane
belief in spacious trust in love.

RECAPTURED

Recaptured, the disaster owns the mind
somehow, interminable due process.
No wonder we should pray for the dead.

No less than this, full disclosure
is needed to trust love's justice.
No wonder catastrophe reigns in every

reportage of Greece, the crack
in Europe's legacy where once
one Aristotle bloomed monastic bunkers.

At least the darkness then could kindle
reason at the site of burning bush.
Tonight the rules of advertising and

the art of propaganda are the text.
One's duty chimes the midnight hour.
Elusive sleep is this life's bedrock.

THE PLOT

The plot involved a parlance of art
and contraband buried in hamburger.
Throw in sex, and the perfect crime

unravels like Cleopatra's carpet.
We are each Julius Caesar here.
Perfect anything has long been killed,

but nights of long knives lurk
for you according to the script.
No calendar predicts the Ides of March.

The butler seems to hold the script,
and lurching from the dream you see
the TV screen across the room that first

is open field and holy icon both.
You roll onto your back. You lost
the chance to read a crucial fact.

TUXEDO

PART II

PASSPORT TO DESTINY

Leave it to English 1944 films
to favor comedies about the bombing.
Elsa Lanchester believes her life is

now charmed by her dead husband's
glass eye. She brings to her committee:
"What would you do if your life was charmed?"

Such Kierkegaard choice provoked
an old woman's rant: "I'd show that Hitler
what for!" And so a mission is born,

to go to Berlin and assassinate Hitler.
The Magic Eye held true through stunts
of English music hall into the SS den.

The deaf and dumb scrub woman
hears and knows all, and finally claims the
shock and awe: "Boys in a blinking raid!"

HUNTING U-BOATS

The solution to aerial hunting of U-boats
was painting plane bellies as blue sky.
Radar found U-boats as cryptologists flagged.

The Battle of the Atlantic scores high
and Shakespeare's tragic logos blinks.
Now Yoko Ono rears as art's assassin,

watching paint dry the truth in trenches,
the last word in suicidal glory's claims.
She anarchized anarchy. She played her part

to bring an end to interminable impasse.
She paved a genre of vampire cartoon lore.
The mop-head boys are in a blinking raid.

Song construction saved the Crown
and everything it means. Rule of law
survives the cataclysm of all things camp.

AN INVENTORY

An inventory then ascends just
as drifting rest in your cave beckons
with recondite fingers. A raven perches.

Its mouth is gaping, but no sound.
The list of chores at God's right hand
is hope of those who die in thee.

Straw must be bundled and forked.
The circus will soon be moving on.
The show is flight without a net

and grand parades of snorting beasts.
It must go on. Jehovah Witnesses
notwithstanding. The chore list breeds

with Darwin's selection intuition
till it wakes you up in a sweat.
Faure's dirge as lullaby is playing.

THE CLOWNS

The clowns, of course, are the Big Top's spine.
These are characters who profile social norms
performed *du jour* in ludicrous mime.

Gone as Brigadoon, the soul of polis,
the comic stunt that speaks, soon forgotten
in contrast to that facing the tiger's terror.

It's mere relief from suspense, history
exiled from philosophy now pretzeled.
Here is deconstruction's noble work,

or would have been if noble clowns
had not been hunted down and buried.
The excavation site is here, if blind spots

given spotlight were the scholar's job.
Most ludicrous, the poet mimes the sleuth
and dons the midnight wisdom mantle.

THESE POCKETS

In an instant of time our nakedness
between regulation sheets could grow
new pockets, selfie-photo casual.

To be "the most interesting man in the world,"
aside from gorgeous women on each arm,
requires prophesy as stark as skin pockets.

Emotion and intellect need a mixing
with all *mysterium* engaged, where
human and divine mix it up through time.

According to the record. And the recipe.
Mixing flavors is the art involved
in entertainment's mandate to amuse,

but these pockets are a miracle of God.
Or Darwin's unintended consequence
of *sacramentum* branding select souls.

MIDNIGHT SOCIETY

Identity theft protection reigns.
You missed your calling, and one you trust
is lucrative and suitably *film noire*.

Now you'd be glad for the final niche
that Groucho Marx found, dangling words
whose secret may be tripped for cash

while facing you, the grouch who's seen
it all, yet sees more every broadcast day.
This could be the perfect last career.

It beats the fate of Robinson Crusoe
with his science of casuistry prearranged
and Man Friday in that jungle tuxedo.

Midnight Society recaptures jazz
and trips the light crescendo cool.
Address change: the inn at world's end.

TONIGHT, CHINA

Internet addiction has struck Red China,
complete with addiction treatment programs.
Is this the iceberg's tip? The treatment

involves the worst Mao revisionism yet.
It could be torn from John Paul II's page,
"Personalism" trained in Bead Counter City.

Person-to-person encounter is a Jurassic Park
that needs your laboratory of test cases,
your captured DNA inside the amber stone.

Your future could have relevance after all.
Heaven's grand collective could tumble
into faithless souls through prayer barrage

and you play Virgil holding tours in Tartarus
for Chinese victims of toxic virtuality.
Tonight, China. Tomorrow, the world!

AT WORLD'S END

At world's end, such comrades stop in
to have a pint and contests of wit that
purgatory could seem a true heaven.

Ownership unites the likes of these.
Their gambits are down payment in
a scheme unspoken, actual possession

by some flagrant insult to death's curse
and unspeakable mercy, creeping arms
of motherhood, landing with final say.

Their antics are exhibit A in plotting
any passage that could only end with Z.
Omega is the space station designed

as mansions of rehab for the likes of you.
What else could bear fruit in this soil?
The dirt at least is sinless, nurture scarce.

OUR GLASSES CLINK

Our glasses clink to dirt's fond friendship
from the first expulsion into life's world.
And nurture is the bond that nets

our daily catch of miracles that scoop
the headlines: ownership actually prospers.
Dirt, the stains of work, the crushing

rocks of fate's humiliations, all ask
for trust in the rubble reason foreordains.
More than research at time's end,

being appointed judge and jury by
alleged divine coercion, labeling souls
like rented tuxedos at Men's Wearhouse,

is not owning the dirt along with our sins.
The twilight makes its usual entrance.
Parzival shrewdly utters: "Sleep on."

TUXEDO

PART III

PORTUGUESE NOSTALGIA (SAUDAJE)

The Portuguese nostalgia predates
every famous claim of golden
age since empire's famous collapse.

But theirs was also nostalgia forward,
Eden as a phantom project both ways,
no angst our moral wasteland provokes.

They had no clue what termites munch
the wood of feral dreams of home
and hearth, what future poisons rule.

That creature known as "man-of-war"
becomes your pet here where the slip
into your mind's fond REM retrieves.

Large bladder-like sac with Gothic crest
topside where sea meets air, a nest,
a floating colony, your charmed beast.

BREWERIES

No closely guarded secrets more
successful than the breweries
extant, per ancient recipes each.

This is evidence that facts exist,
that secrets can be kept, that medals
of award are no flotsam on froth.

The subject, being booze, indeed
is quite confined to matters of taste.
Postmodern critics point to bias

uninformed by reason, this while
raping reason of fact, utility
the end-all truth. Taste is truth,

with all its subjectivity, a fact,
with all the dignity of peat
where bogs preserved the dead.

NOTHING NEW

The abdication of reason is nothing
new, Classic paganism parceling void
between philosophy and religion.

Religion ranges like a beast in heat
while philosophy splits the atom.
Reason is the orphan child of Titans,

divorced before their vows were made.
She roams a disconsolate waif today,
wage-slave made and poor in mulch.

And only Gospel fervor seems to
split unreason's atom into field
of one and only integrated whole.

Reality is soldiering for reason.
This faith is such a leap that only
Soren himself could fathom its risk.

HE FATHOMED

He fathomed how the moment of choice
was a landing strip for vital data,
the needed substitute for tired objectivity,

the useless numinous leap that sings.
He furtively stalked young women
he admired just to make his point.

He fathomed how risk is our true home,
our common landing, our data saved
in substance of Aristotle's anchorage.

Would it were so, and pray it's not.
You'd rather dust off the classics than be
caught dozing on abstract risk disguised

as reason, its home a gladiator's cell.
But he fathomed the singing of the leap,
progress in beauty bounding with good.

SCIENCE FICTION

Teleology of thinking is the tool of true
that's missing from the modern toolbox.
True has become arbitrary appetite,

and all the while denying human nature
as if to do so might offend other species.
Life is a minefield of aimless monads.

No wonder science fiction ascends
while you gratefully wait for robots
to serve you drinks at the formal ball.

You realize you have now fallen asleep.
But you want to be there at the ball,
so you roll over and bask in the mood.

The robots are elusive. Now you want
to find something else. It feels like hope
to search like this. You slide into joy.

A TREASURE LOST

Good is beauty's sidekick here
where bungee cords are optional,
where progress contradicts itself.

It's a daring claim that maybe stumbles
onto good quite wedded to every fact,
a necessary combo courting history.

It's a kind of Lost Ark, refinement
its own reward, distilled in aged wood.
But this grand claim has overlooked

the absence of the instruments of truth.
This is today's ruin we live amid
like monkey's on a Hindu tomb.

This is why young men grab jihad
in homicidal glory since their nature
craves heroic truth, a treasure lost.

MOTHER'S WORD

You've stumbled onto hope's chemistry.
It shuns presumption and thrives in cheer.
Its composition promises ultimate proof.

The waiting room is a robot-free zone.
You depend on the mercy of strangers.
The legend of the Human soaringly plays.

He's said to have broken into nature's doom.
He's said to have met remorse with love.
He's said to have plans to renovate hell.

She sings an aria into this underworld.
She cradles the disconsolate soul of man.
She manifests as signpost to the One.

And gratitude becomes the lasting theme.
You search for trash bags for your pride.
You wake with trust in mother's word.

FUNCTIONAL CONCEPTS

Functional concepts are lighting up
one bulb at a time, beds to make
and tables to set. Who needs a gym?

The climbing flights alone is cardiac.
How brilliant, the "ought" you water
that grows in the soil of Hume's "is,"

defying with color and dash the gloom
of early dawn. The criterion for anything
being what it is, grows from a function.

Every name that Adam passed out
in Eden was the fruit of careful study.
Like arranging the plates and silverware,

second nature with a house you haunt.
Functional is Hamlet's ghost warning
his son of tasks more pressing to come.

HOW BRILLIANT

Excluding functional concepts in arguments
is the test for coherency. But it fails.
Turns out function is blazing "ought" itself.

Intentionality with a mop is personal,
a naming of each board and brick,
a pressing of awards on all you see.

Coherency's name is function's revelation.
The One behind that name is known
far better than anyone, leaving out

the hidden Nazareth years and the
unreported hours in Purgatory. Coherency
is Himself profiled among the dead:

There *you* are, as Light arrives in Hell!
You squint to see that Man from cross to
certain resurrection, and he looks like you.

THE FIVE STEPS
OF THE
ASTRAL MUMMY

.

ASTRAL MUMMY (1)

The blinking, implied command is a flirting orb
of science fiction's imagined seduction, large
in the hypnotic pulsing lights of close encounters.
The interrogation is not, exactly, going well.
Conscience. I'm being told to stop and dig.
(My nails can take it. Dirt just strengthens.)
The alien trap my viscera convulsively rejects
mimes Testament. If only I'd leaned on friends,
Horatio, for example, facing my father's doom.
So I dig, like Ophelia's grave redeems him.
Lourdes has water to confound all alien claims.
Conscience is Enlightenment's most oblique land,
the most opaque, most fugi-covered country.
It's desolate as some Hollywood-rendered blight.
I may end like some astral mummy in Area 54.

FUGI-COVERED COUNTRY (2)

Eyewitnesses observed a transfer of cash that night.
Worse than mummification, disco makes
a comeback on the world stage of my bedroom,
to the point where I woke up planted vertically
and homicidally defiant of invading squirrels.
It began with payola behind giant cacti,
evidence of criminal intent managed. Fugitive
misdirection invites a Bellshazzar's wall.
Intent. Is that really too elusive to prove?
Or have correctness masters murdered all means
of common insight? The borders of this country
are not in dispute. But rule-of-law intent
seems on the lam, here in Fugiland. Witness
Chesterton's Bulgar, on Broadway, "LIVE."
He plants intent where innocence can thrive.

IT HAS BEEN SAID (3)

It has been said that poets have a special
cultic adoration for numbers. Confirmed.
It's the one superstition of content called pagan
making Christian civilization's big-time.
For example, they counted the fish on that beach
in Galilee, post-Resurrection. Votes
apparently count. Confounded naked eyes
doubt nothing of the real in consequence.
One man's real being another's mirage,
let's just focus on the absence of absence first
and call *that* reality, or at least the reality
pertinent to this interval in history's march.
ABSENCE OF ABSENCE FIRST is our slogan
in the long campaign for a nation's redemption.
It's an ugly business, counting smelly fish.

MNEMOSYNE (4)

Memory. It always comes back to a plot
that is bundled by, say, Calliope as gift.
A yeoman's philosophy, this spinning yarns.
What might still be becomes the memory's art.
And nothing really "pure" presents as catholic,
tarnished and grave, finding tribal voice
in the lyric echoes inside that personal cave.
You need to give yourself a good talking to.
You need, they say, to start by being grateful . . .
Maybe moments like this, digging out the Bible,
deserve an epic treatment and not self pity.
If so, we're in luck. Ecclesiastes, for example,
the Book of Convoked Assembly, but absent
the assembly, is opened. It's packing meander-
stones.
Vanity. Its disguises are prancing in Plato's cave.

TALLIED IN THIS BILL (5)

I have seen all things under the sun.
Behold. In wisdom comes sorrow. Knowledge?
Grief. Vanity has chased you to the border.
(This is where good old Bogart usually rescues.)
Film noire, the perfect modern genre, seems held
in disgrace unless anointed by said wisdom.
No gift lightly taken, this tolerance
for grief taught in the Book of Ecclesiastes.
"Grief" includes irritation's last tittle!
The magnitude is not to be dismissed.
Every creepy crawling pursuit of sleep
is tallied in this bill we serve on God.
Calliope's bundle, no midget mummy, even
in the dogma of purgation. Yup.
Don't worry. Blessed, your hands in mind made up.

ROCK 'N RODEO.

LAWDY MISS CLAWDY

I can't live without her.
    The herd gets restless at the thought.
Here's when we sing to calm them,
    to avoid the dreaded stampede.

I can die within her.
    A cowboy song goes New Orleans
and Lawdy Miss Clawdy strikes a chord
    and elusive life slides home.

I can choose her to die within,
    like any knight errant
whose lady's standard is enough
    to face even self extinction.

The dreaded stampede is worst scenario.
    That's why it takes the velvet touch
of, say, Fats Domino to ease in
    before he hammers home my claim.

What have I to lose? Mistress poverty
    is my most faithful consort.
The audience thinks it's she
    whom I should love best.

I could lose what reputation I've earned!
    (Which would hardly be a fortune.)
The audience is with me to go for it.
    Lawdy Miss Clawdy, she's mine.

BEASTLY NEED

Bulldogging steers like some Minoan
    is the cowboy's prime event.
More than riding ill-tempered beasts,
    it's all about grasping horns

and taking all four hooves off ground.
    Interrogation specialists bring
to ground a suspect by becoming
    his last breath of free air.

This is how the falling on the horns
    from horseback strikes a bull.
It's something friendly with a twist.
    Truth is surrender's known quantity.

To be known is alive with need
    in every soul that walks the earth.
The sadness could poison all pools
    to know the crimes that this need breeds.

Interrogation specialists, like cowboys,
    cannot concern themselves with this.
Philosophy is least among their tools.
    Their quest for truth dismisses cause.

Motive is the road map, and the ground
    you count on for confession
is the bull's back delighting in dust.
    You count on beastly need for dirt.

SAINT DENIS

Saint Denis, a.k.a. St. Dionysius,
    250 AD, rode six miles with his
own severed head under his arm,
    that head still proclaiming the Gospel.

The event was more than most rodeos.
    This august cowboy took the belt
for toughest *cephaloros* since the Baptist.
    He's auto mobile though, scene

from Miller's "Misfits," the one that makes
    the last celestial scene make sense.
Clark Gable's drunken rant for his kids
    deserves the badge of Saint Denis.

Each character has his Denisian scene.
    Montjoie! All Fourteen Holy Helpers
who face disease head-on are here
    assembled in a kind of council.

Warrior healers line the ramparts,

    their armpit-carried heads proving

ventriloquism is mastered as fact.

    Everyone says she should run for office.

I've been waiting for Jean d'Arc to show.

    There are more serious tortures,

by some lights, than decapitation.

    The same Gospel applies to all Helpers.

SIDEWAYS LOOKS

The infested call out "Save Us!"
    What herdsman hasn't heard it?
I wish I'd taken up the harmonica.
    They moan about parasites, worse

than your most stubborn itch, your worst
    proctological nightmare, your ears
colonized by implacable fleas.
    Makes ultimate slaughter a mercy.

Who says cowboys aren't philosophers?
    Maybe not in rodeo, where gravity
itself plays such a role occupying mind.
    But on the trail, wisdom soars.

They could be excused for heresies.
    They decide by facts on hand,
discussing thoughts over campfires
    while dealing from fate's deck.

What they have is a field table and time,
    where man as gambler, or any role,
is married to the category "good."
    "Wisdom is counterfeit without it!"

I'm getting sideways looks. Aristotle
    is the cowboy I know would get it.
Aquinas would sum it all up by
    demonstrating Natural Law.

.

HIS NAME

"Save Us" is his name here, scripted
    in various ways in multiple westerns.
The fast gun with conscience reigns.
    The nameless wise drifter rocks.

Gangster rap is no less anonymous,
    more a cry for help than the plume.
But there it is. It's wedged among stones
    and marked to honor an unknown god.

It bends into service obscure cargo
    toward a universal cult of justice.
Vulgarity drifts into wit that saves us.
    The planet seems to rock and roll.

Who else could move our fragile orb
    with deft aplomb so strangely sure.
His riff redeems both pests and herds,
    both crops and swarms, wrestles

any crocodile fools may swim among.
    She is running on his ticket now.
The end of market strangling allies
    with the end of Christian beheading.

Human trafficking's end would be nice.
    How about an end to virgin raping?
Does it take a no-name hero to save us?
    Without her bearing Him, what?

Histrionicus
histrionicus
histrionicus

I am standing waiting for a bus and the young
man standing next to me suddenly says:
"The name of the common wild duck is
Histrionicus histrionicus histrionicus." There is
no problem as to the meaning of the sentence
he uttered: the problem is, how to answer . . .

Alasdiar MacIntyre
After Virtue

LIKE GENERAL GEORGE AND CRAZY HORSE

There's a point at which history
   tires of repeating itself.

The narrative is suddenly held hostage
   to some novelty again, already

where disgust is just. New ones simply
   must drive home to the old lessons

with fresh ears toward unrestricted mind!

There's a Eurotopian paradigm jewel,
   a horse of a different color, a strong horse

where idealism counts most, and unto death.
   Here's the horse on which to put down odds!

If civilization is just too big to fail,
   still blunders have me spurning bulletins.

Like General George and Crazy Horse, even
   bullets seem useless facing such crocodiles.

STRONG HORSE, DARK HORSE

Hooves, dust flying, propel a signature moment.
    Benedictus snuck in at the last possible pulse.

Truth be known, he disgraced himself.
    He flattered potential investors shamelessly,

all that his dubious stamp should somehow endure.
    It seems to me a last chance contestant

could be more humble, grateful he still breathes!

But that's I, the perfect sample of grammar, doing
    Grandma proud with my deft reports.

Excellence focused. Telescopes and microscopes.
    This just in: "The lens in competition

has not yet reached the status of Hubble."
    The drag is from bureaucrats counting beans.

And the crocodiles are not yet tagged and filed!
    What? You thought there'd be progress?

NEVER MIND

Never mind the crocodiles. We'll assume
    what is royally spoken by the mob prevails.

That could be a good thing or a bad thing.
    And here we are again pondering the difference.

I submit that it is not unlike forensic investigation,
    this calling to connect real dots for a change.

Let's *tabula rasa* the whole proposition. Survival

is not the last claim on virtue that humans earn!
    (Now it's time to admire the Grand Canyon.)

Where do we start? We start where amusement
    has some chance of approaching Jane Austen

with philosophy's garlands, truth be known.
    Justice, as usual, claims center stage,

and we keep on scrambling that hash that passes
    for poison gas wherever juries convene.

WHO KNEW?

Who knew that populations could
    self-extinct from reaching
growth capacity? Demonstrated in
    culture dishes and empty prairies.
But Malthus be damned! That nonsense
    exposes itself forensically
if only the right questions find a space.

A space like that would be truly riveting.
    You'd take off your hat to it,
that melodious exhibition of original thought.
    Political correctness demands
we not name it as it is: The uniquely human.
    This would be "speciesism."
And naming your enemies is also frowned on,
    unless it's that defenseless Cretan, "Man,"

earning "the environment's" pink slip,
    a Guy Fawkes on a long fuse.

PRIZES

Legends of the Jersey Devil are more convincing.
    At least in the tale of its chimney escape

with subsequent stranger at the door, if furtive,
    proves your *benedictus*, your one

of many more lucky streaks yet to come!
    Limit for such as we is the backhand shot,

the come and go of things, our Waterloo omega!

Wind currents sailed upon with humor's wings!
    Seriousness about humor could be a mistake. . .

There are common sense limits. But nothing targets us
    like some asteroid or flunky jihad plot.

The stranger prizes discovery in limits. What thwarts
    is really the frolicking gown, screen-tested,

unfurling the narrative artists know, but managers
    label big-footed Yetis planting phony footprints.

LITERALLY COMBUST

"Break a leg!" Now there's a cliché, a flotsam
    of cheap literary value 'til the stage enters

with context, burning need, the way a Vermeer
    mundane scene can literally combust you

with flights of devotion unfulfilled, beauty,
    with all its Hamlet-joys, lest God alone

keep you on your feet facing crisis-world.

And here we are, toes pointed toward footlights.
    Who woke up Coleridge for this triviality?

At least *he'd* sign up for this common-speak!
    As long as the gypsy sees no pentagram on

my palm, the one I wave with, I trust that merit
    would be spotted flopping laundrywise.

But clichés possess a place in a rogues' gallery,
    a no-fly list known for its editorial stamp.

ENTHRALLED

It is a beneficent calling to assert
    a randomness theory without going over

to the dark side like evil-cousin-anarchists.
    I just want to claim my mule and half-acre.

And I have. Randomness has steered me well,
    avoiding Bogart's prospector pitfall.

That last laugh! Enthralled! Tiny human will!

It's a wild side, a knee slapper. A doctrine?
    Al contrario, it's a spousal declamation.

The wit actually matched the solemnity! And as
    treasure treks go, this one demarcated well

how Aristotle is no "turnspit" with a dirty dog
    on a treadmill hooked to *my* grand rotisserie.

What he lacked in the great claims of history,
    histrionicus quacked in starlight navigation.

THE
CAPRICCIO
SONNETS
PART I

CAPRICCIO

Yes, it can grow thick hair on balding heads.
Disease can never faze prosaic play
when tripped fantastic. Others only fled
the lurid guise of innovation's day
like mitochondria reverting back
to primal anaerobic funk. The Calf
of Gold awaits the tablets of attack.
So obvious, I simply had to laugh.
Capaciousness is bad. Capricious, good.
It cures the common cold and cancer both.
Its world-stage saga, hear me, truly should
be recognized, that telescopic oath
that Hubble now fulfills announced today:
a solar system prize light years away.

ONE'S OWN BROOD

If waters by the shores of Babylon
can help one spot the great blue heron's flight,
you'd think that Pound's own demiurge, upon
the Nietzshean modern purge, the future bright,
had more than deck chairs rearranged. Old news.
Not news with splendid truth enshrined in facts
but propaganda, phony facts. The blues.
That one-note-Charlie "Legion" levies tax!
The other thing of certainty is death.
No deck chairs rearranged help sight the wings
the heron could unfold to catch your breath.
No singularity or Black Hole brings
an appetite for light and solid food
and wisdom for the lives of one's own brood.

TEMPTATION

Temptation. There's where nakedness can count
as some endurance test between the odds
and free will's claim as wisdom's only fount.
If all you need is love, why well placed pods
near somnolence? Is nakedness our food?
So, call it candor, call it racing blood,
or call it liberty from things tabooed.
A child recites the coming of The Flood
that prophesies the next in text: The Flames.
Our worldly types demur. Reality,
for them, is endless space and taking names.
The company we kept, East India Tea,
for instance, passed the steepest modern test
of works transgressive at its very best!

TRAGICAL DOCTOR

Like Marlowe's trag'cal Doctor Faustus, I
could growl out midnight conjuration of,
say, Alexander or my Helen, buy
their insubstantial acts of hand in glove
with this poor misfit soul whom Christ redeemed.
The one so tragical I conjure here
and now, for what it's worth, and how it seemed
transparent with opacity, I fear
is way beside the point. The Doctor's in.
It's true, his soul is hacked by secret moles.
He calls for research into what is sin
while Mephistopheles keeps shoveling coals.
Each soul confronts the tragical and just
and must decide between the gold and dust.

INLAND TREASURE

Capriccio is demonstrated by
phenomena within the natural world.
The documented studies can't say why
cross-species partnerships succeed, have squirreled
away a lasting bond, while colonies
of coral polyps, same species, make war.
Or how a species learns. I must say, please,
don't give us Darwin's ever-limping bore.
Explain instead the spectacle, unique
across the globe, when dolphins, at low tide,
up Carolina estuaries, seek
an inland treasure. And the local pride
of inland birds confer. Then dolphins herd
a flopping catch on bank: shared feast. Absurd!

DEPLORABLES

When twenty-three paired chromosomes arrived
on gusts of March sonatas blowing through
her seamless garment of a soul, alive
and poised for April's sprouting, tried and true
as pollination: Woman at the Well.
It took her only wisdom to believe,
clairvoyance helping things. But no hard sell,
no brazen miracles that day achieved
its well-spring to this broad outside the pale.
Deplorables, elites have made it clear:
Your twenty-three paired chromosomes will fail.
And yet mere uttering from good is dear
to you, excites a fear in you, brings cheer
to know the Son of Man is finally here.

ONE'S FORTITUDE

How bold is bold? The question of the day.
The question of each moment of a choice
is always such. One's fortitude can fray,
or worse, seek no more risk than flags to hoist.
Not symbols nor the semaphore of good
intentions is sufficient. Arcane rules,
dry bones, that army of connected "should"
we trust to have our back, are only schools
of fish that synchronize evasive "could."
Our taking risks would presuppose a spine
in Body Politic, not skulls of wood
or knives on Ides of March the bottom line.
O righteous Bruti, may I say, "*et tu.*"
On *your* hands is the blood of virtue's crew.

REALMS OF TONES

". . . one solely breathes in realms of tones," she said
of music, Clara Schumann, genius, saint
if truth be told, if life be truly led
by charity and joy without complaint,
an outward fact that one can breathe, must breathe
with all the senses. Accidents or guise
mean nothing as emotions strongly seethe
for country where the best in beauty lies.
Like Eucharistic wonder, every tone
within the mind finds correlation here,
inside the world as is, a world alone
but for the many tones that sternly steer
the ship of thought into a glee of light
within a sea of utter witless fright.

EACH CHAPTER

Each chapter seems to birth the world anew!
Aeneas flees a burning Troy, and twins
abandoned to the wolves somehow imbue
a future in empyrean where sins
find Sabine truce, historic compromise.
Begins the Pax Romana. Chapter two.
But let's not dwell on massacres, and lies
that brought the noble to their knees and flew
the banner of injustice once again.
The chapter when a monk called Bede showed true
intention proved the might of history's pen!
But how can nature seem to have no clue?
Dark ages lurk in every sprouting bud
and fertilize all life through winter's mud.

THE GIFT OF TORPOR

The high speed helic-arcing wings that hum
like monks among the lilies of the field,
or Chaucer's twirling tongue with the aplomb
that you'd expect from language deftly sealed,
the hover of the smallest bird astounds.
Its feather's iridescence edifies
the eyes, the colors startle. Hope abounds
that somehow mid flight mating-dancing flies
into the face of someone born to nest.
But like most pilgrims, worst of all, the dour
threat of nightfall for this breed whose rest
from feeding can't exceed the quarter hour.
For such as these the gift of torpor is
the silent acrobatics, *mute* show-biz.

#BAMBOOZLED

Bamboozled is the word that I now use
in making sense of shallow roots and trunks
of hollow, narrow, brittle social views.
Utopians, both left and right, are punks.
They claim a bamboo paradise where rot
is quite quotidian. Half-toppled trees
in density that strangles life is not
a hashtag with a message one could seize
but more like marking time on prison walls.
Look, nothing less than hyperphatic glance
down Being's Tree like prayer that slowly crawls
before it learns to walk and finally dance
can plant the grove of heaven's kingdom come.
For now bring out your dead and beat the drum.

SCHRÖDINGER'S CAT

How cats appear so often to the mind
as object lessons of heuristic trope
by, now, even the quantum theory kind,
is worth reflecting on by this bold dope.
Reflecting is itself the central theme,
a Gilgamesh before the flood. And here
is Observation, savage sidekick, dream
of "all" and "any," quantum field, no/a queer
wave function forcing every ending rhyme.
The cat inside the box is dead, but quick
before you lift the lid and see how time
and observation dictates nature's pick.
The cat is dead. Long live the flaming cat.
Schrödinger's crouched and poised to chase his hat.

HYPERBOLE PETRARCHAN

When death at one's own hand is meant as joke
like Beatles' lyrics touting a warm gun
or saying that you almost had a stroke,
hyperbole Petrarchan has its fun.
The humanist approach to things was worth
its weight in seesaw thrills, Platonic scoop
in Aristotle's cone, sprinkled with mirth.
The *"buone lettere"* was born to swoop
through pounding Occidental hooves into
a tolerance for absentminded whim.
The photo finish shows by nose who flew
into the poet's mind as houselights dim.
Who wants to hold his nose on Judgment Day?
Petrarch has claimed his laurels history's way.

DIET OF WORMS

For good or evil ends, the prisoner's itch
became gestation for "The Book," deployed
like deadly flying drone on that of which
the author calls corrosion unalloyed,
like Luther's shrill appeal for purity
of faith inside the diet of the worms.
No "veritable Pic," encyclopedic, he,
but versatile in all Renaissance terms.
He would have loved our moving picture shows,
projection on our cave's opposite wall.
From our cave, Luther might have thought he knows
a fearful truth pertaining to Man's Fall.
From our diet of worms he might have scratched
emancipation's book before it hatched.

THE
CAPRICCIO
SONNETS
PART II

THE SONG OF THE VENETIAN GONDOLIER

One owes an homage to the past when nerves
can count for steady tillage in these swamps,
where Mendelssohn wrote "Gondolier," who serves
up abstract "Song," (no "Voice" as such) no romps
in sacks to humanize the dirge: then BLAST!
Old Armageddon doom in woodwinds! Bring
to bear the truth of what on earth won't last
and how the end won't see the nations sing. . .
But what could last on earth is worth a thought.
This earth of ours is pushed by GABRIEL's pole!
So let's not jump into the froth not sought.
Our sloth alone prevents the Judas role. . .
We're one ahead, and gaining with each lap.
The trumpet we obey's not evil's trap.

.

BUGS OUT THERE

A lot of bugs out there. The Temple Mount
is all that's left of targets one stampedes
from plagues that storm the battlements that count
as Western Wall. The bugs breed in the weeds.
Venetian democratic grandeur, more
an institution one should recognize
than has been seen as worthy for.
The list of holy sites would try for size,
would breed with glee in tunnels of the mulch,
would claim some squatters rights on theme.
But that won't do. The ambush at the gulch
is *faite acompli* if you don't have a scheme.
Momento mori is the orb I grasp.
My liberty supreme is this next gasp.

INVITATION TO A VOYAGE

"abundant, calm, voluptuous. . ." Oh damn!
That Baudelaire, he knew the art of love,
the gift of summoning the perfect man
for every woman's voyage, wand to dove,
sweet coins behind the ears, endearments sprung
from knowledge only poet's have. It's true.
The old man proved it. Beats an anthem sung.
Say, who competes with "the whole town," his blue
of Oriental splendor heaven-rung?
He plays *olfactus* sax to rouse her nerves. . .
Most interesting, he does it with one lung!
An anthem, not preferred in rousing, serves
the crown of love, the homage due at end.
The perfect one you seek is your best friend.

MYSTERY OF INIQUITY

Then witchcraft walked into the wedding hall
as bride of science, pregnant with the "-mancies,"
conceived by "bundling's" hygiene, winter's wall.
A divination in discernment fancies
how our pilgrim fathers charted rounds,
and handshakes meant intent. And Granvill thrusts
"Plus Ultra" on some Rosicrucian grounds
into the place where reason always rusts.
You'd root, romantically, for magic's way,
but science was New England's champion.
Iniquity is foul intent! Obey
when lipid oxidation is no fun.
Since common sense can do quite well in fog:
The occult bride of science, queen from frog!

BEFORE I LEARNED TO READ

Look, I was there before I learned to read.
You might say Descartes' axiom is here,
the place for mythic fulcrums, conscience freed
from history's burdens. That's when nature's cheer
allows reflection. Barry, friend from fields
of battle. We were there before the oath.
Or were we? Never mind. The point: it wields
strong data for support of native *ofthfff*.
The weight of birth, the manifest of new
as universal dogma conscience-bound.
Do we not staff friend Plato's "Band of True"?
What warrants Socrates on site as clown?!
Before we learned to read we saw the way
in daily lessons, measured. Limits play.

UNLETTERED CHILD

Unlettered child, you'd plundered ocean tales
and secrets long before you learned to read.
Just larynx sonic alphabet. Say whales?
A dream recalled: my inner Moby freed
to swim the fertile sea lanes with no dreams
because in whaledom every dream is now:
that plaintive, haunting song. Routine. It seems
to me, asleep and dreaming, *knowing's* how
I locate pitch. That spot. You know it well.
It makes us friends to glean such pearls before
the world of print had cast capacious spell.
Let harmony's caprice, like Gauguin's snore,
remind us of those days of childish lore
when shell games and a song were what's in store.

EVIL'S TRAP

Evil's trap is not the bugle's call
to loyalty. That call is virtue's prize
to one for whom philosophy is all.
The only noise that evil makes is lies,
with megaphones when meant to foster fear.
It kind of creeps, a silent scaly noose.
T'would close all options. Evil. Trap it here,
with virtue's noose! This is where the loose
and cavalier gets old. Side-choosing time.
The lure for this trap must be Goodness nailed
to every tree on earth, the perfect crime
of mercy either dared or chicken-failed.
High noon's the protocol for last words said.
Then evil dies like leaven farts from bread.

SYMPATHY FOR CICERO

Poor Cicero survived to see his Rome,
Republic and the rule of law, wiped out,
the state reduced to tyrants' whims. His home,
his life, was gone, what folk songs sing about,
(like certain Tarot cards or Bible quote:
". . .for Christ" I teeter *praecipit* with dog
that leaps at heels and barks with savage throat.)
But what in truth it meant for him, the slog
in endless quicksand, slave to justice priced
on merely passing schemes, is something more.
With no explicit knowledge of the Christ,
his intuition scored. Consoled, the door
of death and failure slid where best enticed.
The Moulin Rouge reprise is sliced and diced.

MOULIN ROUGE REPRISE

Those big-eared weeds are insolent and crude
along the walkway to the creek, not flat
against the ground like yesterday, or glued
to drumbeat red alerts, now perky. . . Brats!
All betting I won't bring to bear my scythe.
A festival of weeds is launched, unless
this poem interferes with edicts blithe
and quite imperative with warrants stressed.
We'll see. Old Cicero would build a case.
Perry Mason-style. Toulouse would sound
for wire color, line, and flag that race
as cabaret. Exuberance is found!
They say the work of art is never done.
If so, I may just have to get my gun.

WAR FOOTING

Rapacious globalism packs the meat.
It now requires anti-missile strikes
by missiles to maintain a table seat.
The last are first, we're told. So Holland's dykes
are plugged to 'nth degree, commando style.
War is more than geometric play.
It's *the* unfathomable natural law, no guile
and flirting through first date, spare parts the way
to measure victory. A Tokyo Rose
for every veteran of this cursed war!
Spare parts collide with daring plan. The coals
are stoking in this battle cruiser. Core
beliefs are on alert to silence, friend.
And only then, geometry I send.

LA BAGATELLE

Without that molecule this man would be
someone who haunts in shadows of disease,
what prone elites despair of, honest key
to anything unlocking life well pleased.
Just see how experts seal their expert fate.
But there was an anointing no one saw,
like David's furtive moment, shepherd's gate
the standard that the molecule can draw
on every up-and-coming slingshot planned.
Not planned in geometric finitude.
It's, in the main, not true his flight's not manned,
(which testimony seems to now include.)
It's planned beyond derangement, in the fact
that bagatelles owe little to past act.

THE BEST PART

The question is the protocols to land.
And that would seem the nub of this, the code
that unlocks colonizing, something grand,
at Texas scale, with eyes upon your road
defends non-contradiction's silly law
as manifest in landing's needed plan.
Not least, you keep in mind, the plan will draw
from research gained, your brain true string-on-can.
A cyber datum's rescued from the Web!
You'd say it's kind of Carnival, the bells
and lights to bring on seizure, now celeb
with stories never told of nudes from shells.
"You leave your glasses where you lost your heart"
sings chorus as she taxis, the best part.

DR. SWIFT

Now, Dr. Swift (of Gulliver fame) had fun.
He coined as noble "sweetness" paired with "light,"
with diction thrice restrained. The first race run
is plain ideas astonishingly bright,
declarative and readymade. The next,
in simulcast, is pomp and pride cum Pope's
Augustan sense, true grit for sculpting text.
The last restraint arrests all far-fetched tropes.
Like sonic slaves we bind ourselves to sound.
Far worse than formal challenges still lurk
in Nemo's ocean leagues ahead. Come 'round
emancipated soul. No fear of work.
The call to action's where I'd like to end,
the coin of mutineers I'd like to spend.

SO HERE

In light of revelations: *capriccio*,
I'd like this chance to summarize a bit.
So rare, this face-to-face, with time in tow
at crucial moment when the truth is it.
I want the air of recitative that wails.
I want the force of words to baptize all
into the death that saves us. If what fails
requires showing up for curtain call,
I'd say to take a bow since who can tell
what is unique from you or gift of God?
Don't think the shamans don't effluve bad smell.
Reading animal entrails finds the odd
Carl Jung explored. But it stinks too. So here,
my bagatelle, my spare-parts scene, my cheer!

AUTHOR'S NOTES

on the

TUXEDO

COLLECTION

INTRODUCTION

Providing author's notes on a work *in* the book, *for* the book with a road map (and justice for all), this has not been tried since T. S. Eliot as far as I know. This is largely because it's generally agreed that submitting one's own self critique (before the carrion critics descend) is bad form, a violation of the valid principle that "the work" must stand on its own. And besides, is this guy claiming to be another Eliot? I've put on the table my reasons for reluctance to include this author's "notes" with this *Tuxedo* volume of poetry. There are two reasons why I've overcome my bashfulness. The first is that friends and family have applauded this idea, having long since campaigned for it. The second is because of something that the composer Berlioz set as a precedent. For his *Symphonie Fantastique,* which debuted in Rome in 1830, he provided written program notes "linking the movements with verbiage to form a story." (*From Dawn to Decadence,* Jacques Barzun.) It was well suited to the birth of Romanticism in Europe to provide programmatic authorial supplements to works of art. And we in the US are long overdue for the birth of a new-Romanticism. Therefore, these notes actually are a manifesto that represents cutting-edge practice!

THE *TUXEDO* POEMS

Divided into three parts, nine poems in each part, totaling twenty-seven sequentially intended poems is the opening gambit of the volume called *Tuxedo*. Each separate poem has fifteen lines arranged in five triads each. It speaks of order, of the measured intentionality that separates poetry from prose. But in the case of this work, the signal flashed for order is not so much the comforting rhymes and lilting meter of, say, a sonnet. (See the closing collection of twenty-eight sonnets for comparison.) This is free verse. It's free, yet it abides in an organic-seeming order of its own. Like in an Easter egg hunt, discovering evidence of order is part of the fun of this kind of poem. I would say it's a work of new-Romanticism. It tells a story. It has that passion in a twilight atmosphere. But I get ahead of myself. My job here is to show how to evaluate a poem the way you might purchase produce. First you handle it, squeeze it, and smell it. Even the darkest poem can prove ripe and the brightest bruised.

Some folks just don't like romanticism, period. Other poem cycles in this volume are much more expressionistic, more upbeat in tempo and less "programmatic" than the *Tuxedo* poems. But that makes them ideal to unveil. All I have to do is point out how the speaker in the poem (think of him as Coleridge's "Ancient Mariner") seems to never leave his bed for the duration of twenty-seven poems. One way or another, he is always struggling to fall asleep or fitfully dreaming, his only apparent contact with the outside world coming from the TV in the background. It may take the reader another poem or two before catching on that this guy must be suffering from either post traumatic stress or sees himself in some dire jeopardy.

That first line of the first poem, where he's stretched out in bed as an infant being sung to by, presumably, his mother, initially disguises a more sinister scene figured in "sleep's shadows" where "loss and hope" wrestle in the subconscious. This lullaby he regresses to, himself swaddled, could also be that last helplessness in a hospice bed. Yes, you're old enough to know the truth. The lyrical lullaby of your glorious infancy is waiting in your last breath. Each line of the poem is terse and matter-of-fact. He reports to us: "The catastrophe you earned" has brought "solace in nakedness" from this mother or nurse who has never promised him a "future grand tuxedo." For him his life is reduced to spasmodic clutching at mobiles dangling in his face. The one ray of light in this prediction of doom is the suggestion that his report, indeed the poem, may amount to some kind of "founding research."

These verses are no cold-blooded analysis, despite how emotionally muted the narrator seems to be.

This tone of almost robotic flat affect is consistent with trauma victims. And as listeners to this story, we sense much seething emotion underneath his pronouncements. Meanwhile, the specter of a disembodied tuxedo is stalking him in a world where "cruel masquerade is fun." This is the *leit motif* of the journey on which the narrator takes us into the mind's underworld.

If you notice anything in all this handling of the produce, it should be how all the poems are written in the second person. While we take for granted that the "you" deployed throughout is the one who speaks, this device has the subtle effect of underscoring a possible trauma-induced disassociation. At the same time, the "you" could be understood as addressing the listener. This device projects a snugness, an intimacy of universal suggestiveness in his magical mystery bed.

I would understand if someone asked to know what trauma in my biography triggered *Tuxedo*. If I told you I'd have to kill you. I mean that in the same way as the Zen injunction to kill the Buddha if you meet him on the road. Reductionism is not the artist's way. It's not that I wouldn't gossip with you over drinks about all the triggers of all the works. But it would not further the appreciation of any true work of art. It's about appreciating the lapidary fashioning of many mansions of resonance, that leaning into universals with particular (original) evocative industry. That's the ticket. By the grace of God. That's the ambition. A journey with the doppelgänger Tuxedo, being haunted by an empty suit, suggests ambivalence about issues of personal success. It also conjures images of post-imperialist guilt and James Bond swagger. Or it's the dreaded uniform of subservience. And of course, it also speaks to life's formal celebrations. Look at that first poem. Maybe the "she" who sings the lullaby at your cradle didn't promise you a grand tuxedo, but instead promised that whether at harvest or in dirge, a transcendent consolation will suffice.

Not to give away the ending, but "the world as mattress" staging of these successive poems offers an endless platform on which to hold forth on all of my pet peeves in life and our society with impunity, because I'm making art. After I've glossed Western civilization from that mattress, which is actually my favorite part, these poems will actually satisfy the good old American preference for a dramatic climax. So I can promise, even if "she" can't, that the "he" who calls himself "you" will have a happy ending to all his convalescent mutterings to himself. I could boast that the happy ending described in *Tuxedo* will be a surprise ending, surpassing the expectations of even those who know how Catholic I am, how Catholicism infuses my work like "the Buddha" infused the American Transcendentalists. If you follow my tack.

Yes, a surprise ending awaits you. Especially my Catholic friends. They might be the only ones with the theology to get the full implications of the twist at the last scene. This reminds me. I wanted to point out that, unlike the time of Eliot, when a poem cites an obscure reference, we are only an icon away from an instant rundown. So I won't be going from poem to poem analyzing each historical reference, much less symbols and metaphors. Multiple associations are always welcome.

THE FIVE STEPS OF THE ASTRAL MUMMY

These five poems are an appendage to *Tuxedo*, a sort of tail more than a tale. (Note here a more "symbolist" strategy of poem-making as compared to the romanticism of *Tuxedo*) This mummy must lurch up five more steps to recovery. We find the same poet finally out of bed but now prisoner in a room. Let's admit this is progress. Our protagonist in *Tuxedo* was last seen in Purgatory. That leaves a lot of room for mummy-walking. We find him under some kind of interrogation. He's speaking to us in the first person. He's awake. He's swatting at his conscience. He thinks he sees aliens. By the second step, "Fugi-Covered Country," he's in his room "planted vertically/ and homicidally defiant of invading squirrels." But in this prophetic state of madness, wisdom starts bubbling up. It's not just invading rodents, it's those elite fugitives, the "correctness masters," claiming the special privilege of immunity. Suddenly we can't find "intent" behind actual proof of destroying evidence? Free will has been suspended for a top-ranking political hack!? It's a miracle!

Yes, these five poems were heavily influenced by the events of the 2016 primary and election campaign in these our beloved United States. Yes, not only elections matter, but poetry mixed up in politics matters. At least it often has. These poems, influenced by the Southwest atmosphere in the cable video series "Breaking Bad," are a conscious, if furtive, polemic on current events. It verges on ranting. The "five steps" begin with "I may end like some astral mummy in Area 54." It ends with "Don't worry. Blessed, your hands in mind made up." I wonder what political lever my main character pulls with those hands in his mind made up.

Footnote:

The first poem, "Astral Mummy" ends referring to "Area 54" as the mummy's tomb. I do know that the location of the famous alleged alien body in Roswell was called Area 51. Early in the next poem, it says: "Worse than mummification, disco makes/ a comeback on the world stage of my bedroom." That veiled reference to the famous New York disco Studio 54 actually got a laugh when I first read it to a group of Chestertonians around a bonfire. Which I first took that they got the joke, how I'd deliberately saved that wrong number so I could detonate the joke remotely, in retrospect, a delayed joke. Mainly, I preferred how "fifty-four" sounds. The number "54" is funny! 51 is *not* funny. Simple as that. So, awkward or not, I'm keeping it. Doing something as daring as that is romanticism's spirit!

Of all times on earth, striking the Byronic pose seems most appropriate for all the space we've earned ourselves as a civilization. Romanticism is a movement that has distinct and intriguing parameters that I claim are exactly who we are in today's version of modernism. We're even liberated by the Byronic triumph of endless characterizations of that darling fugitive self in its dramatic and brilliant portrayals telecast over cable, just to mention one demonstration of romanticism's endurance. Even our hip-hop style of stratosphere is also nothing more than the Byronic pose. And why not? Let's come out of the closet.

As regards produce handling, notice how these five poems are less concerned with signaling "order," in all that apparent free-wheeling verse, than in sustaining dramatic monologue's internal order, restraint below the radar. Fifteen lines, again, for each poem. But not divided into pastoral-seeming triads. The lines just barrel through like a platoon of tanks. Each line, however, is rigorously measured in the traditional five emphasized syllables per line. But the rhythmic pattern is shaped only according to how I, Emperor of France and Literature, believe the line would actually be said (on stage, as it were.)

ROCK 'N RODEO

I call these my cowboy poems. There is a sudden shift in mood
from dark pondering to playful sunlight as we emerge from the
mummy tracking. In my youth I'd studied art appreciation at the
famous Barnes Foundation in Merion, Pennsylvania, instruction
led by Miss Violette de Mazia herself, Dr. Barnes's closest
colleague. Right now she would be pointing out, using the actual
paintings, the difference between the murky, dark drama of the
Venetian masters versus the vivid, light-filled, Florentine style of
painting. These cowboy poems are in the Florentine tradition.
Handling these poems, you'll note a big role for playfulness less
apparent in the previous ones. In my own handling, I take a delight
in the "decorative" intentionality (as compared to the more
"illustrative" intention of the *Tuxedo* poems.) I remember as a kid,
back before my burning bush beckoned, the Beatles astounded me.
And I did not want to like them. But I liked, among others, how
when each new song hit the radio waves, "originality" seemed to
just plant its flag in my ear. When told it was a new Beatle song,
instantly, of course! Who else would be so original? That stamp of
the original is something that for me migrates sideways, exploring
new pathways, unafraid. My first resolve has been to avoid

endlessly repeating myself.

After declaring my rule to avoid autobiography in these Notes, here I've been revealing my faith, my politics, and even founding encounters. At this point I might as well share one more thing, how only half of me points north to the Delaware Valley. On my mother's side I'm Texan. We're talking Comanche and twister and dust-bowl survivor Texan. The impulse for a simple ballad to praise a gal gets diverted into calming the cattle-drive herd. The scene shifts back and forth between the cattle drive and a debut in New Orleans of a Fats Domino song. The second poem in this, another five-poem series, discusses the virtues of bulldogging steers at the rodeo. It's noted in the poem that, like in police interrogation of a criminal offender, the steer secretly wants to be brought to the ground. How do you do it? By becoming "his last breath of free air." The cowboy trail has so far revealed that "Truth is surrender's known quantity" and that we can "count on beastly need for dirt." And how "wisdom soars" on the trail, society's deplorables camped and playing cards. Someone shouts: "Does it take a no-name hero to save us?" (Or did the cattle moan that sentiment?) The narrator quietly comments: "Vulgarity drifts into wit and saves us. The planet seems to rock and roll."

This almost decoratively styled series of poems, thinking of Matisse on the Texas frontier, reminds me of how our most ancient Classical ancestors understood virtue as mainly constituting courage.

HISTRIONICUS HISTRIONICUS HISTRIONICUS

These seven poems, also consecutively intended, are among the most "expressive" (as compared to being mainly decorative or illustrative) of my works. If the book *Tuxedo* were a symphony, this would be the movement I'd designate as *allegro vivace*. And I think that the content, philosophically, is as ambitious as its tempo. Epistemology, always a crowd-pleaser, actually reigns here.

I've decided to refuse the temptation to dissect this series of poems in any way. I leave it to the reader to perform these poems "for" and "to" him or herself, and I leave to the critics the exploration into any occult secrets. Anyone who has come this far should by now have all the means to prosper among this flock where my quacking signals echo in these verses. But I did promise you a guide to each "movement." So here is my advice. When you read this series, imagine that you were just elected president of the United States, and that you're giving a public speech that becomes your most intimate sounding of one's country ever. Imagine that Western civilization is consequently at stake.

THE *CAPRICCIO* SONNETS

The final sequence of poems in *Tuxedo* is twenty-eight sonnets, written sequentially but not necessarily to be read in sequence. Having already contributed sonnets to two other of my books, one of which was comprised entirely of sonnets, these last twenty-eight poems complete my bucket-list goal of matching Shakespeare's lifetime record of 154 sonnets. Now I can die.

There is the thread of a narrative running through these *Capriccio* sonnets. The first poem establishes the virtue of "caprice" over "capaciousness." And the thread of this analysis, with nature and history feuding along the musical bass line, recurs in different forms and extends onto the *leit motif* that extols the virtues of this category of spirit: "*capriccio*." The word itself signifies a type of musical composition that is playful, seemingly glib, but also can be deeply complicated in disturbing and unseen ways. Capaciousness, on the other hand, aside from representing the bottomless pit of human desire and depravity, signifies for the speaker the terrifying emptiness of outer space. "*Capriccio*" is alleged in these sonnets as the antidote to that dreaded disease: "capaciousness." It claims to be the eagerly sought for elixir of youth, a Northwest Passage, a third way that grows hair. The Byronic pose.

ABOUT THE AUTHOR

Award-winning American poet and performer Tad Cornell (T.
H. Cornell) was essentially an underground poet after his first
book, *Glance Over at These Creatures,* was published in 1977.
Some of his poetry was distributed conventionally, but more was
personally bound and hand-gifted, presented in poetry slams and
avant garde stage productions (in Hong Kong, Houston, and
Philadelphia), and on guitar and vocals as part of poetry fusion
rock band, Edgar Allen and the Poettes, and other ensembles.

Cornell's childhood until age twelve was in Germany where his
father worked for the US State Department (as a CIA agent, Cornell
later learned). He was a child opera star at the Frankfurt Playhouse, and
studied theater and wrote music in high school in suburban Philadelphia.
During three semesters at Goddard College, he was inspired to pursue
poetry by Paul Nelson. Cornell earned a BA in English from Temple
University, a master's degree in special education from Antioch College,
and a master's degree in English literature from Villanova University.
The special needs of his only child, born with spina bifida, led him to a
thirty-year career in social work. At intervals along the way, he was
drawn to consider the priesthood, served as a Trappist novice in the
Abbey of the Genesee, and studied theology in Rome at the Angelicum.

OTHER WORK BY TAD CORNELL

The Needle's Eye (Juggling Teacups Press, 2016)

Blue Heron Rising (Juggling Teacups Press, 2015)

In Whom Is My Delight (Juggling Teacups Press, 2015)

The Unspeakable Mating (Latitudes Press, 1989)

Honey From the Rock & Hong Kong Elegies (Latitudes Press, 1988)

Glance Over at These Creatures (RHD, 1977)

CHAPBOOKS

The Graphics of the Mouth (2006)

Gloria Über Alles with Stan Heleva (script and score, 1999)

It Seems Important (1988)

The Promise of Silence (1978)

Rosie Knuckles Knows (1978)

Cough Poems for the Tickle (1978)

Looking the Moon in the Face (1977)

Hollywood Diamond Exchange (1977)

Marco Polo (1977)

www.ingramcontent.com/pod-product-compliance
Lightning Source LLC
LaVergne TN
LVHW021523080426
835509LV00018B/2636